D0824778

# SOME MAJOR EVENTS IN WORLD WAR II

## THE EUROPEAN THEATER

**1939** SEPTEMBER—Germany invades Poland; Great Britain, France, Australia, & New Zealand declare war on Germany; Battle of the Atlantic begins. NOVEMBER—Russia invades Finland.

**1940** APRIL—Germany invades Denmark & Norway. MAY—Germany invades Belgium, Luxembourg, & The Netherlands; British forces retreat to Dunkirk and escape to England. JUNE—Italy declares war on Britain & France; France surrenders to Germany. JULY—Battle of Britain begins. SEPTEMBER—Italy invades Egypt; Germany, Italy, & Japan form the Axis countries. OCTOBER—Italy invades Greece. NOVEMBER—Battle of Britain over. DECEMBER—Britain attacks Italy in North Africa.

**1941** JANUARY—Allies take Tobruk. FEBRUARY—Rommel arrives at Tripoli. APRIL—Germany invades Greece & Yugoslavia. JUNE—Allies are in Syria; Germany invades Russia. JULY—Russia joins Allies. AUGUST—Germans capture Kiev. OCTOBER—Germany reaches Moscow. DECEMBER—Germans retreat from Moscow; Japan attacks Pearl Harbor; United States enters war against Axis nations.

**1942** MAY—first British bomber attack on Cologne. JUNE—Germans take Tobruk. SEPTEMBER—Battle of Stalingrad begins. OCTOBER—Battle of El Alamein begins. NOVEMBER—Allies recapture Tobruk; Russians counterattack at Stalingrad.

**1943** JANUARY—Allies take Tripoli. FEBRUARY—German troops at Stalingrad surrender. APRIL—revolt of Warsaw Ghetto Jews begins. MAY—German and Italian resistance in North Africa is over; their troops surrender in Tunisia; Warsaw Ghetto revolt is put down by Germany. JULY—allies invade Sicily; Mussolini put in prison. SEPTEMBER—Allies land in Italy; Italians surrender; Germans occupy Rome; Mussolini rescued by Germany. OCTOBER—Allies capture Naples; Italy declares war on Germany. NOVEMBER—Russians recapture Kiev.

**1944** JANUARY—Allies land at Anzio. JUNE—Rome falls to Allies; Allies land in Normandy (D-Day). JULY—assassination attempt on Hitler fails. AUGUST—Allies land in southern France. SEPTEMBER—Brussels freed. OCTOBER—Athens liberated. DECEMBER—Battle of the Bulge.

**1945** JANUARY—Russians free Warsaw. FEBRUARY—Dresden bombed. APRIL—Americans take Belsen and Buchenwald concentration camps; Russians free Vienna; Russians take over Berlin; Mussolini killed; Hitler commits suicide. MAY—Germany surrenders; Goering captured.

## THE PACIFIC THEATER

**1940** SEPTEMBER—Japan joins Axis nations Germany & Italy.

**1941** APRIL—Russia & Japan sign neutrality pact. DECEMBER—Japanese launch attacks against Pearl Harbor, Hong Kong, the Philippines, & Malaya; United States and Allied nations declare war on Japan; China declares war on Japan, Germany, & Italy; Japan takes over Guam, Wake Island, & Hong Kong; Japan attacks Burma.

**1942** JANUARY—Japan takes over Manila; Japan invades Dutch East Indies. FEBRUARY—Japan takes over Singapore; Battle of the Java Sea. APRIL—Japanese overrun Bataan. MAY—Japan takes Mandalay; Allied forces in Philippines surrender to Japan; Japan takes Corregidor; Battle of the Coral Sea. JUNE—Battle of Midway; Japan occupies Aleutian Islands. AUGUST—United States invades Guadalcanal in the Solomon Islands.

**1943** FEBRUARY—Guadalcanal taken by U.S. Marines. MARCH—Japanese begin to retreat in China. APRIL—Yamamoto shot down by U.S. Air Force. MAY—U.S. troops take Aleutian Islands back from Japan. JUNE—Allied troops land in New Guinea. NOVEMBER—U.S. Marines invade Bougainville & Tarawa.

**1944** FEBRUARY—Truk liberated. JUNE—Saipan attacked by United States. JULY—battle for Guam begins. OCTOBER—U.S. troops invade Philippines; Battle of Leyte Gulf won by Allies.

**1945** JANUARY—Luzon taken; Burma Road won back. MARCH—Iwo Jima freed. APRIL—Okinawa attacked by U.S. troops; President Franklin Roosevelt dies; Harry S. Truman becomes president. JUNE—United States takes Okinawa. AUGUST—atomic bomb dropped on Hiroshima; Russia declares war on Japan; atomic bomb dropped on Nagasaki. SEPTEMBER—Japan surrenders.

# WORLD AT WAR

# Battle of Okinawa

# WORLD AT WAR

# Battle of Okinawa

By R. Conrad Stein

Consultant:
Professor Robert L. Messer, Ph.D.
Department of History
University of Illinois, Chicago

 CHILDRENS PRESS ™

CHICAGO

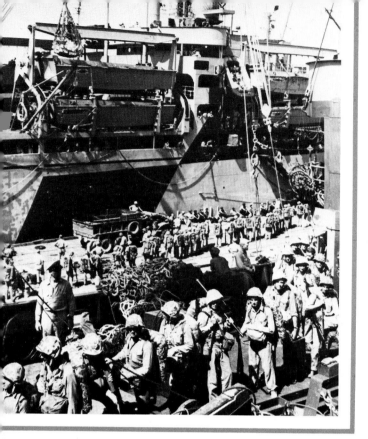

Preparation for the American invasion of Okinawa is underway as marines board troop transports at a base in the Pacific.

**Library of Congress Cataloging in Publication Data**

Stein, R. Conrad.
 Battle of Okinawa.

 (World at war)
 Includes index.
 Summary: Describes the desperate struggle between American and Japanese forces for mastery of the Pacific island Okinawa towards the end of World War II.
 1. World War, 1939–1945—Campaigns—Japan Okinawa Island—Juvenile literature.  2. Okinawa Island (Japan)—History—Juvenile literature.  [1. World War, 1939–1945—Campaigns—Japan—Okinawa Island.  2. Okinawa Island (Japan)—History]  I. Title.  II. Series.
 D767.99.045S74   1985    940.54′26    85-10970
 ISBN 0-516-04765-5

FRONTISPIECE:
An American soldier cares for three Okinawan children who were found hiding in caves.

PICTURE CREDITS:
NATIONAL ARCHIVES: Cover, pages 9, 21, 30, 33, 41 (bottom)
UPI: Pages 4, 6, 10 (top), 12, 15 (top), 17, 22, 24, 28 (bottom), 31 (top), 38, 40, 41 (top), 42, 43, 45, 46
WIDE WORLD PHOTOS: Pages 10 (bottom), 15 (bottom), 16, 18, 23, 27, 28 (top), 31 (bottom), 34, 37, 44

COVER PHOTO:
Spotting a Japanese cave hideout, an American soldier shows his partner where to aim his flamethrower.

PROJECT EDITOR:
Joan Downing

CREATIVE DIRECTOR:
Margrit Fiddle

Task Force Fifty-eight was the mightiest fleet ever to sail the Pacific. The fleet was assembled in late 1944, when many new warships were joining the United States Navy. Its job was to turn the Pacific Ocean into what the Romans once called *mare nostrum*—our sea. In ancient times, no enemy dared challenge the Roman fleet on the Mediterranean Sea. Certainly, Task Force Fifty-eight was powerful enough to make the Pacific an American *mare nostrum*. It consisted of sixteen fast aircraft carriers, eight new battleships, fourteen sleek cruisers, and forty or fifty destroyers. This mighty collection of ships swept the Pacific, demonstrating America's power wherever it sailed.

In Japan, the once-powerful Imperial Navy was in shambles. Her carriers and most of her battleships and cruisers had been sunk. But the Japanese had one desperate "weapon" left. They had hundreds of young fliers who were willing to crash their airplanes into enemy ships. They were the *kamikaze* pilots. Their motto was: "One plane, one warship."

The suicide planes were a menace to all Allied shipping, even the powerful Task Force Fifty-eight. In early 1945, five of the task force's carriers were damaged by air strikes. Despite swarms of defending fighter planes and furious barrages of antiaircraft fire, the determined Japanese fliers still managed to score hits on the big ships. Task Force Fifty-eight was safe from enemy planes only when sailing at cruising speed. Then Japanese aircraft, including the deadly kamikazes, had a difficult time finding it. But when the fleet had to operate in the same waters for days or weeks at a time, enemy fliers could easily locate the ships.

A Task Force Fifty-eight fleet carrier burns after being struck by a kamikaze (suicide plane). The Japanese relied more and more heavily on such suicide missions as they neared defeat.

In March, 1945, Task Force Fifty-eight joined a large group of transport and other ships to support landing operations on the Japanese-held island of Okinawa. Naval commanders hoped the battle for Okinawa would be brief so the ships of the task force could return quickly to the high seas.

Before landing on Okinawa, the United States Navy bombarded the island with fire from planes and offshore gunboats. During this preinvasion strike, smoke billowed from the dock area of Naha, Okinawa's capital city (left), and a landing craft launched rockets toward the beach (below).

The invasion fleet at Okinawa was immense. Some thirteen hundred ships bobbed in the waves near the island. Gunboats shelled the island for days. A navy man named Edward Higgins gave this description of the bombardment: ". . . the fire support drummed a thunderous tattoo. . . 20 and 40mm quads [four-barreled machine guns] and .50-caliber machine guns pumping in perfect rhythm as they fired . . . at the beach. Behind them destroyers worked back and forth . . . slamming three and five-inch shells in arithmetic patterns into the jungle above the shoreline. Beyond the destroyers were the cruisers and battlewagons salvoing their six, eight, and sixteen-inch guns in great bursts of fire that made their land targets jump and shiver, erupting in clouds of dust and debris."

As part of the preinvasion assault, American carrier planes bombed this Japanese shipping and installation site at the mouth of a river.

On Okinawa, some hundred thousand Japanese soldiers waited. Most crouched in caves dug deep into the earth. The caves trembled as heavy shells exploded above them. Commanding the Japanese was a clever general named Mitsuru Ushijima. General Ushijima was a soft-spoken man who liked to write poetry in the late evening hours. In his heart, Ushijima knew that Japan would lose the war.

But he intended to make the enemy pay for its final victory. One of the orders Ushijima issued to his men was this: "Fight to the last and die for the eternal cause of loyalty to the emperor."

Most Japanese soldiers, sailors, and airmen believed that death was preferable to defeat. Because they were so willing to die, the Pacific War grew bloodier as it dragged on. Wars usually intensify in their later stages. In 1945, the fighting in the Pacific had grown particularly desperate. The Americans had been engaged in a long campaign called "island hopping." That meant leapfrogging from one island to another while building up staging areas for the assault on Japan. The island of Okinawa was the last stepping-stone on the island-hopping program. It was only 1,000 miles from Tokyo, 450 miles from the mainland of Japan, and less than 100 miles from Japan's southernmost islands. The Japanese defending Okinawa were prepared to fight as desperately as if they were defending the soil of Japan.

From United States fleet headquarters came the command: LAND THE LANDING FORCE. The date was April 1, 1945. It was Easter Sunday—a strange day to begin an invasion.

A thousand yards from the beaches, giant doors on landing ships yawned open. Landing craft called amphtracs splashed out. Each amphtrac carried about twenty-five marines or soldiers. In long lines they churned toward the beaches on their tanklike caterpillar treads. Many of the men on board the amphtracs were veterans of half a dozen previous landings. Some had assaulted the tiny atoll of Tarawa, where hundreds of marines were killed before they were able to move even a hundred yards inland.

Left: The invasion of Okinawa began as amphtracs churned toward the beaches on April 1, 1945. Below: A beachhead was established on the southwest coast of the island. The supporting fleet offshore included destroyers, cruisers, and battlewagons.

The first Americans to hit the beaches were surprised to find that they met no Japanese opposition and were able to advance inland standing up.

But on Okinawa the men found the beaches to be strangely silent. Admiral Richmond Kelly Turner, in charge of the landings, was astonished. He radioed to headquarters: "Troops advancing inland standing up." By nightfall, about sixty thousand soldiers and marines had landed. There had been almost no casualties.

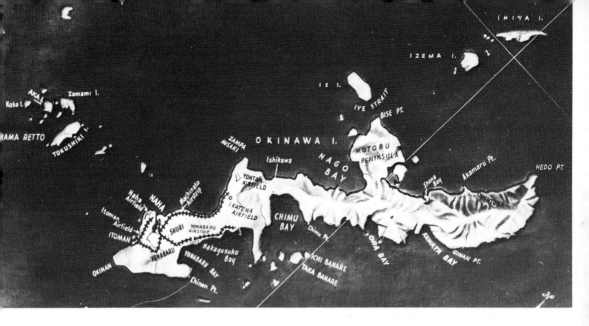

Allowing the Americans to land without a fight was part of Ushijima's strategy. General Ushijima knew that the big guns on American ships would blast apart any defenses the Japanese tried to establish near the beaches. So Ushijima conceded the beaches and most of the island to the Americans. Okinawa is about sixty miles long and varies between three and twenty miles in width. Ushijima decided to defend only the southern third of the island. He hoped to hang onto his portion of the island and make sure the battle for Okinawa would be a long one.

A long battle would keep American ships floating offshore. There they could be found easily by Japanese airplanes taking off from bases in southern Japan.

A kamikaze dives straight for an American warship.

On the very first day of the landings, kamikaze planes struck the fleet. One suicide plane crashed into the British carrier *Indefatigable*. An officer on board her wrote, "The Jap aircraft came straight for the *Indefatigable* from five thousand to six thousand feet and passed over her to the starboard. It then pulled straight up and looped over the top to come down vertically into the ship. I imagine the pilot intended to down the funnel [smokestack], but missed and hit the flight deck."

The Allies would soon have to fight another, far larger suicide craft.

In Japan, the largest battleship in the world left port to steam toward Okinawa. The *Yamato* was on the most incredible suicide mission of the war. The giant battleship carried only enough fuel to make a one-way trip to Okinawa. The *Yamato* had orders to wade into the Allied fleet and sink as many other ships as possible before being sunk herself. If she were not sunk, the ship was to be driven onto the beach and was to keep firing until there were no more shells to fire. The battleship's orders read: "The fate of our empire truly rests upon this one action. . . . Each unit will harden its resolve to fight gloriously to the death to completely destroy the enemy fleet."

The *Yamato* was an awesome battleship. She was twice as large as most American battleships and was armed with nine 18.1-inch guns. Even the biggest battleships in the United States fleet carried only 16-inch guns. The *Yamato*'s guns could hurl a 3,200-pound shell a distance of twenty-two miles. But admirals and ship designers always seem to be preparing to fight the previous war. During World War I, in which battleships had fought other battleships broadside-to-broadside, the *Yamato* would have been invincible. Most World War II sea battles, however, were fought by carrier planes, and opposing ships rarely came within sight of one another. The *Yamato* had yet to be a factor in any battle of the Pacific War.

Sailing toward Okinawa, the battleship and her accompanying cruisers were spotted by two American submarines. The submarines radioed a warning to Okinawa. Planes scrambled off the decks of the carriers of Task Force Fifty-eight. The mighty *Yamato* never got to within two hundred miles of the Allied fleet.

On board the superbattleship came the shout, "Enemy planes off the port side!" Japanese antiaircraft crews readied their guns. But the gunners were inexperienced. Most veteran Japanese gunners had been killed during previous battles. American pilots quickly penetrated the barrage of Japanese antiaircraft fire. Two bombs tore into the *Yamato*'s deck. A

The Japanese battleship *Yamato*, the largest battleship ever built, was sent on a one-way suicide mission to Okinawa.

torpedo ripped into her side. But the *Yamato* had thick armor plating. When she was launched in 1941, the Japanese navy had called her unsinkable. A second wave of American planes attacked the battleship. They bombed, torpedoed, and raked the ship with machine-gun fire. Scores of men topside were killed. Their twisted bodies lay on the deck. After a dozen hits from both bombs and torpedoes, the end finally came to the *Yamato*. She listed to port, keeled over, and disappeared under the waves.

Dead and wounded sailors dotted the water where the *Yamato* once had been. On its mission to Okinawa, the great ship carried a crew of 3,332 men. Only 269 survived.

Americans in tanks advance across the fertile terrain of Okinawa.

Four American divisions—two marine and two army—had landed on the beach at Okinawa. The marines moved north and the army pushed south. For the first week, they met no real resistance. The marines had been accustomed to fighting over small coral atolls such as Tarawa and Iwo Jima. Those sandy, almost treeless, dots in the sea had very small native populations. But Okinawa was a fertile island on which there lived nearly half a million people. Rice paddies and tiny farms made checkerboard patterns on the landscape.

General Simon Bolivar Buckner, commander of the United States land forces on Okinawa (left), strides along an Okinawa road with General Roy S. Geiger.

Commanding the American land forces was General Simon Bolivar Buckner. His father had been a Confederate army hero during the American Civil War. Buckner was known to be tough. While stationed in Alaska, he had developed the hobby of hunting the savage Kodiak bear. Certainly Buckner had no love for his enemy. During the war he had adopted a favorite toast. With guests, he often raised his glass and said, "May you walk in the ashes of Tokyo."

A kamikaze plunges into the water after being diverted from its target by American antiaircraft gunners. During the Okinawa campaign, American naval forces absorbed 1,465 Japanese air attacks.

At sea, furious battles raged between the United States Navy and the Japanese kamikaze pilots. The Japanese had been launching organized kamikaze attacks since late 1944. But during the Okinawa battle, they came in waves of one hundred to three hundred planes.

The word *kamikaze* means "divine wind." In ancient times, it was said that a "divine wind" had swept down to destroy an enemy invasion fleet that was approaching Japan. In 1945, the Japanese hoped that a new divine wind would save their country.

American navy men found the suicide pilots to be both frightening and fascinating. On a ship off Okinawa, American Admiral C. R. Brown wrote, "We watched each plunging kamikaze with the detached horror of one witnessing a terrible spectacle rather than as the intended victim. We forgot self for a moment as we groped hopelessly for the thoughts of that other man up there."

Who were these men so willing to die? Rumors abounded among the Americans. The kamikaze pilots were drugged. They were drunk. They were religious fanatics. They were not really men at all, just cleverly made robots.

In truth, dying for the cause of their country was something most Japanese soldiers were willing to do—even if that meant piloting a suicide plane. It had been drummed into the Japanese since boyhood that dying for the emperor was glorious. The kamikaze pilots had simply chosen a particularly spectacular way to die a "glorious" death.

Yasunori Aoki was a twenty-one-year-old kamikaze pilot. He loved nature and had studied forestry at college. As the day for his mission approached, he had second thoughts about giving up his life. He once looked at a fly buzzing about a windowpane and said aloud, "How lucky you are to be alive." But on the morning of his mission, Aoki said his prayers and wrote letters to his family. To his younger brother he wrote, "Our divine country will not be destroyed." Many kamikaze planes were manned by a crew of two—a pilot and a navigator. Aoki served as navigator. He and his pilot were lucky. They reached the huge fleet off Okinawa without being attacked by enemy fighter planes. Then suddenly, antiaircraft fire jolted Aoki's craft. Aoki ordered his pilot to dive into an American destroyer. Watching the destroyer loom larger and larger in the sea, Aoki waited for death. He felt

Like Yasunori Aoki, this Japanese suicide pilot (center left) fell into the sea just short of his target.

nothing. His pilot had missed the target. Like many members of the kamikaze corps, the pilot had had little training as a fighter. The plane splashed into the water. Miraculously, the two bombs it carried did not explode, and both men were unhurt. They were later fished out of the sea by sailors from the same ship they had intended to destroy. Aoki spent the rest of the war as a prisoner.

Determined to hold out
against the Americans
as long as possible,
the Japanese defended
their position on
southern Okinawa from
a honeycomb of caves
in the hills.
Right: A marine aims
a flamethrower at the
opening of a Japanese
cave hideout.
Below: Two soldiers
cautiously approach
several cave entrances.

On land, the Americans met stiff resistance. They discovered that the hills to the south were honeycombed with caves held by the Japanese. At one point, a United States tank fired half a dozen smoke shells into the entrance of one of the caves. The amazed tank crew soon saw smoke puffing out of thirty other cave entrances.

Manning positions in the caves were General Ushijima's determined soldiers. Sometimes the soldiers fought in what the Americans called spider holes. These were foxholes with lids. Like trapdoor spiders, the Japanese popped out of the spider holes, fired at the Americans, and disappeared again. Also dug deep into the ground were Japanese heavy artillery pieces and shells. The Americans believed in matching firepower with firepower. Their huge artillery pieces pounded the Japanese positions. But the enemy guns were so well dug in that they could resist the bombardment.

After throwing explosives into a cave, American soldiers lie in wait for any Japanese who attempt to escape from the flames.

General Buckner discovered that Okinawa would be a long, bloody battle. Gains would be measured in yards of ground, and every yard would cost lives. This battle was unfolding exactly as the Japanese had planned. General Ushijima had been ordered to hold out as long as possible. While American troops were fighting on land, they had to have a fleet of ships to support them. And while that fleet remained offshore, the Japanese suicide pilots could find them.

The battle became a
grueling, inch-by-
inch ordeal.
Left: American
soldiers advancing
toward the city of
Shuri use a ladder
to bridge a gulch.
Below: Marines in
a flamethrowing tank
wipe out opposition
along the road
to Naha.

To better destroy enemy ships, the Japanese developed a piloted bomb. They called it an *ohka* (cherry blossom). The *ohkas* were rocket-propelled cylinders with two stubby wings. They were carried to battle strapped under two-engine bombers. Upon approaching an American ship, a suicide pilot would slip out of the bomb bay of the airplane and climb into the cockpit of the *ohka*. The bomber would then release the *ohka*. The suicide pilot would start the rocket motor, and try to steer his craft into an American ship. While the rocket-propelled *ohka* arrowed toward its target, it could reach the dazzling speed of six hundred miles per hour. Americans called the piloted bomb a *baka* (stupid) bomb because they thought the pilot had to be stupid to get into one. But the *ohkas*, packed with explosives, caused terror throughout the fleet. The destroyer *Mannert L. Abele* was hit squarely by an *ohka*. It broke in two and sank almost instantly.

Some Japanese suicide fliers sped to their deaths on rocket-propelled bombs called *ohkas*.

The best way to stop the Japanese air attacks was to shoot down the planes before they could reach the ships. The Americans kept hundreds of fighter planes in the air at all times. In the water, they surrounded their fleet with radar-equipped pocket destroyers. Many kamikazes were knocked out of the sky before they even saw an enemy vessel. But a few always managed to slip through the defenses. As the battle wore on, Allied ship losses mounted.

The American soldiers on this ridge near Naha battled for forty-eight
hours before gaining any ground.

On the island, bitter fighting continued for
weeks, then months. The American navy grew
impatient with the progress of the ground war.
The commander of Task Force Fifty-eight
wanted to get his fast ships back on the high
seas. But the ground troops had to have the
support of the big guns and carrier planes of
the fleet.

Two significant events of World War II occurred while the Battle of Okinawa raged. In Washington, on April 12, President Franklin Delano Roosevelt died. When the Japanese on Okinawa learned of the American president's death, they scattered leaflets from bursting shells over the American lines. The leaflets read: "The dreadful loss that led your late leader to death will make you orphans on this island. The Japanese Special Assault Force [kamikazes] will sink your vessels to the last destroyer." And in Europe, on May 8, Germany surrendered. Hitler had shot himself in his bunker and the Russians had overrun Berlin. The Japanese knew that meant the Allies would soon be able to transfer thousands of men and tons of material to the Pacific. They wrote no leaflets about the fall of Germany.

A major obstacle in the ground struggle for Okinawa was a mound of earth the Americans called Sugar Loaf Hill. Like an anthill, it was interlaced with Japanese caves and bunkers.

One of the marines who fought his way up Sugar Loaf Hill was a sergeant named William Manchester. Later, Manchester became a famous writer. Many years after the battle, he wrote about that awful hill on Okinawa: "Infantry couldn't advance. Every weapon was tried: tanks, Long Toms, rockets, napalm, smoke, naval gunfire, aircraft. None of them worked. If anything, the enemy's hold on the heights grew stronger. The Japanese artillery never seemed to let up, and every night Ushijima sent fresh troops up his side of the hill." Like many young men, William Manchester had joined the marines hoping to find glory in war. But, he wrote, "On Sugar Loaf. . . I realized that something within me, long ailing, had expired. Although I would continue to do the job, performing as the hired gun, I now knew that banners and swords, ruffles and flourishes, bugles and drums, the whole rigmarole, eventually ended in squalor."

In Okinawa, young American soldiers who had expected to find glory in war found only death and destruction. Above: A Navy hospital corpsman administers blood plasma to a wounded Marine. The plasma bottle hangs from a rifle thrust into the ground. Below: After a long struggle to gain control of a strategic hill, some exhausted soldiers are finally able to catch some sleep on an embankment near the front lines.

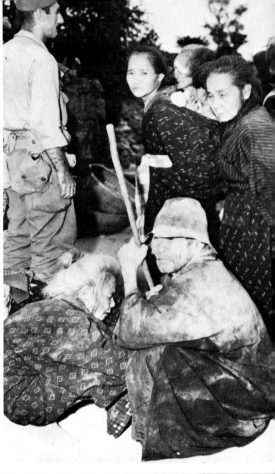

Okinawa's civilians became innocent victims of the war. Thousands were killed in the fighting, and the destruction of the island left many more starving and homeless.

The half million civilians on Okinawa suffered along with the two armies. Most Okinawans lived on the southern part of the island. This was exactly the area Ushijima had chosen to defend. Thousands of civilians—including children and old people—were killed. More than a quarter of a million civilians were homeless and starving at the end of the battle.

After almost three grinding months, the Americans advanced to the point where the Japanese were fighting with their backs to the sea. For both sides, the cost in lives was staggering.

On June 17, with the battle in its third month, a Japanese infantryman delivered a letter to General Ushijima. The letter had been air-dropped over Japanese lines. It came from General Buckner. It read: "The forces under your command have fought bravely and well, and your infantry tactics have merited the respect of your opponents. . . . Like myself, you are an infantry general long schooled and practiced in infantry warfare. . . . I believe, therefore, that you understand as clearly as I, that the destruction of all Japanese resistance on the island is merely a matter of days. . . ." The letter was a request for surrender. Ushijima chuckled over it. He was a samurai. A samurai warrior preferred death to surrender.

The day after Ushijima read the letter, General Buckner climbed down from a hill where he had been observing a battle. An enemy shell burst overhead. Buckner fell, and was dead in minutes. He was the highest-ranking American officer killed in combat during the Pacific War. Three days later, Ushijima crawled out of his cave and committed suicide by thrusting a knife into his stomach. Perhaps his last thoughts were about the enormous civilian casualties he had helped inflict on the Okinawan people. According to a witness, his last words were, "The Okinawans must resent me."

American infantrymen carry a wounded Okinawan civilian to safety.

At the end of May,
Japanese defenses in
the southern part of
the island collapsed.
The fall of "Conical
Hill" (left) was one
event that cleared the
way for the assault on
the Japanese stronghold
of Shuri. The city of
Naha (below) was left
smoking and strewn
with debris after being
leveled by American
bombardment.

Although the American advance was slowed considerably when heavy May rains turned the battlefield into a thick sea of mud (above), the Japanese lines were officially broken on May 31. Throughout June, the Americans conducted mopping-up operations (below) to seek out any remaining Japanese who refused to surrender.

In the last days of the battle, several Japanese soldiers,
one of them carrying a white flag, surrender to United States
Marines. Okinawa was the last major land battle of World War II.

By the end of June, 1945, the Battle of
Okinawa was over. For both the victor and the
vanquished, it had been the bloodiest contest of
the Pacific War. Okinawa cost the Americans
12,529 men killed or missing in action. More
than 30,000 Americans were wounded, and
20,000 suffered from what was called battle
fatigue. At sea, 34 American ships had been
sunk, and 368 damaged. The Japanese lost
110,000 troops. Civilian deaths were estimated
at 75,000.

After the war, the Okinawan people quickly rebuilt their island.

Today, Okinawa is the bustling island home of almost a million people. Neon lights its cities at night and fast-food restaurants line its highways. American and Japanese men who once fought there sometimes return to see what the island looks like today. William Manchester, writer and onetime marine, visited Okinawa in the late 1970s. He climbed Sugar Loaf Hill. He reached the top and later wrote,

Okinawa was the bloodiest battle of the Pacific War. These American soldiers visit a cemetery in Okinawa to look for the graves of friends killed in action.

"I take a deep breath, suddenly realizing that the last time I was here anyone standing where I now stand would have had a life expectancy of about seven seconds. Today, the ascent of Sugar Loaf takes a few minutes. In 1945, it took ten days and cost 7,547 marine casualties."

At the top of Sugar Loaf Hill Mr. Manchester relived the horror and pain of the battle he had fought in thirty-five years before. As he remembered the many friends he had lost, he thought of a prayer he had learned as a boy: "... *take away this murdering hate and give us thine own eternal love.*"

This small Okinawan cemetery contains the graves of fourteen young Okinawans who joined the Japanese army in order to help defend their island.

# Index

*Page numbers in boldface type indicate illustrations.*

*About the Author*

Mr. Stein was born and grew up in Chicago. At eighteen he enlisted in the Marine Corps where he served three years. He was a sergeant at discharge. He later received a B.A. in history from the University of Illinois and an M.F.A. from the University of Guanajuato in Mexico.

Although he served in the Marines, Mr. Stein believes that wars are a dreadful waste of human life. He agrees with a statement once uttered by Benjamin Franklin: "There never was a good war or a bad peace." But wars are all too much a part of human history. Mr. Stein hopes that some day there will be no more wars to write about.